secrets
for
MEN

J. Donald Walters

Hardbound edition, first printing 1993

Copyright 1993
J. Donald Walters

Illustrations copyright 1993
Crystal Clarity, Publishers

ISBN 1-56589-045-0

PRINTED IN HONG KONG

14618 Tyler Foote Road, Nevada City, CA 95959
1 (800) 424-1055

seed thought is offered for every day of the month. Begin a day at the appropriate date. Repeat the saying several times: first out loud, then softly, then in a whisper, and then only mentally. With each repetition, allow the words to become absorbed ever more deeply into your subconscious. Thus, gradually, you will acquire as complete an understanding as one might gain from a year's course in the subject. At this point, indeed, the truths set forth here will have become your own.

Keep the book open at the pertinent page throughout the day. Refer to it occasionally during moments of leisure. Relate the saying as often as possible to real situations in your life.

Then at night, before you go to bed, repeat the thought several times more. While falling asleep, carry the words into your subconscious, absorbing their positive influence into your whole being. Let it become thereby an integral part of your normal consciousness.

Give others freedom to be themselves. Make demands of yourself, but be sensitive when making demands of others.

P

lace more reliance on the power

of thought than on physical strength.

DAY 3

Think for

yourself. Don't

let others do

your thinking

for you.

Don't drive others. Lead them

sensitively to your point of view.

DAY 5

Be strong in yourself, that you may give strength to others. Be like a spreading oak, in whose shade many can find shelter.

Be a sincere friend to all. See

yourself as the servant of all.

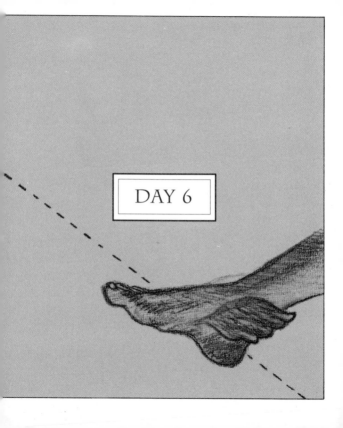

DAY 6

DAY 7

Strive for excellence in everything you do. Seek it not in competition with others, but as a thing to be achieved in itself.

Live always by the truth. Give your word sparingly, but, once it is given, remain faithful to it in the teeth of a hurricane. Where there is truthfulness, there is victory.

DAY 8

DAY 9

Don't take yourself too seriously. There's a world out there, much greater than you are. Flow with its flow, and, like a surfboard rider, know the power that lifts and carries you as greater than your own.

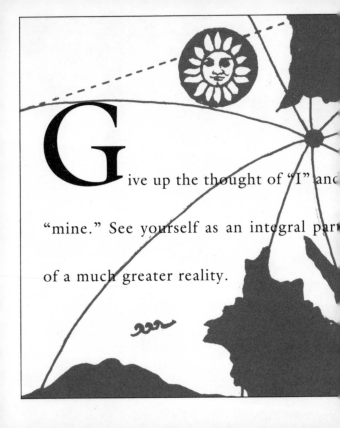

Give up the thought of "I" and "mine." See yourself as an integral part of a much greater reality.

DAY 10

DAY 11

Temper the sword of reason in the fire of practicality. Ask of any idea, not that it be reasonable, merely, but above all that it work.

Don't be relentless in your logic, for logic is only one way of arriving at the truth, and truth itself always transcends logic. Don't allow yourself to be persuaded by reason alone. If reason is to be a friend, it must be guided by intuition.

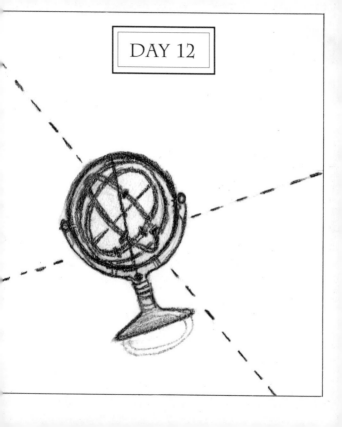

DAY 12

Develop intuitive reasoning by feeling in your heart whether your premise is right or wrong. Remove yourself somewhat from the opinions of others.

Don't use logic as a means of bullying people. Offer it kindly, as a means of clarifying the issues under discussion.

DAY 14

In any discussion, be impartial. Let truth be your guide, not the desire for victory. Indeed, see truth itself as the only victory worth winning.

Kindness and consideration are marks of inner strength, not of weakness. Consider fairly other points of view than your own. Remember, self-conquest is the greatest victory.

DAY 16

DAY 17

Be strong at your center, gentle

.t your periphery.

Inner strength, in men especially, depends far more than most realize on sexual self-control. Consider self-control, not self-indulgence, the mark of your masculinity.

DAY 18

DAY 19

To transmute sexual energy, feel it flowing constantly up the spine from the base to the brain. There is much joy in this practice.

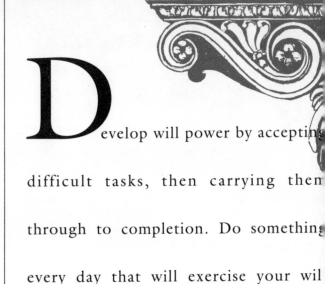

Develop will power by accepting difficult tasks, then carrying them through to completion. Do something every day that will exercise your will power.

DAY 20

Don't be afraid to follow your

own star, even though it shine for no

one else.

*S*trengthen your magnetism by the depth of your own commitment, not by imposing your will on others.

DAY 22

Be like a pine tree, your roots fixed

firmly in the earth, your aspirations rising

high into the sky of lofty ideals.

Let joy be the final goal of all your actions.

DAY 24

Be magnanimous in victory; calm, self-contained, and ever hopeful in defeat. Allow no defeat ever to define your reality, and defeat itself will become a kind of victory.

Respect others, if you want them to respect you.

DAY 26

DAY 27

Develop graciousness and appreciation. These are marks of a refined nature. To cede points to others is to win them as your friends.

Develop enthusiasm for what you do. Reason without heart, though abstractly persuasive, is like an autumn leaf: beautiful perhaps, but at the same time lifeless.

DAY 28

DAY 29

Be inspired by love, but ruled

above all by truth, never by emotions.

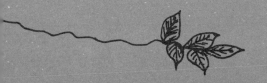

llow your heart's natural love to unfold by renouncing selfishness, self-righteousness, and pride.

DAY 30

DAY 31

Expand the love you feel for your

own to include all others as your own.

Other Books in the **Secrets** Series
by J. Donald Walters

Secrets of Happiness
Secrets of Friendship
Secrets of Inner Peace
Secrets of Success
Secrets of Love
Secrets for Women

Coming Soon:
Secrets of Prosperity
Secrets of Leadership
Secrets of Self-Acceptance
Secrets of Winning People
Secrets of Radiant Health and Well-Being

Selected Other Titles
by J. Donald Walters

The Art of Supportive Leadership
        (book, audio, video)
How to Spiritualize Your Marriage
Education for Life
Money Magnetism
The Path (the autobiography of J. Donald Walters)

Ask for these titles at your local bookstore.

For a free catalog of these books and other selections, please fill out the opposite side of this card, and send to Crystal Clarity, Publishers, 14618 Tyler Foote Road, Nevada City, CA 95959, or call 1-800-424-1055.

I just read _____
title of book

and loved it. I bought it at _____
name of store

in _____
city, state, zip

☐ Please send me your complete catalog of books,
audios, and videos.

☐ Please add my name to your mailing list.

Name _____

Address _____

City _____ State _____ Zip _____

Phone _____
Daytime   Evening